BOSTON

A Photographic Journey

TEXT: **Bill Harris**

CAPTIONS: **Pauline Graham**

DESIGNED BY: **Teddy Hartshorn**

EDITORIAL: **Jane Adams and Pauline Graham**

PRODUCTION: **Ruth Arthur and David Proffit**

DIRECTOR OF PRODUCTION: **Gerald Hughes**

DIRECTOR OF PUBLISHING: **David Gibbon**

CLB 2503
© 1990 Colour Library Books Ltd., Godalming, Surrey, England.
All rights reserved.
This 1991 edition published by Crescent Books,
distributed by Outlet Book Company, Inc., a Random House Company,
225 Park Avenue South, New York, New York 10003.
Printed and bound in Hong Kong.
ISBN 0 517 01494 7
8 7 6 5 4 3 2

BOSTON

A Photographic Journey

Text by
BILL HARRIS

CRESCENT BOOKS
NEW YORK

A few years ago, inspired by the success of the British television series *Upstairs Downstairs*, CBS Television produced a series of its own called *Beacon Hill*.

The setting was Boston in the 1920s, and no expense was spared to make it historically accurate. Costumes were checked and rechecked against museum collections. Accents were refined to be just right. Antiques were brought in at great expense. The series was even filmed on Beacon Hill, using the exterior of 89 Mount Vernon Street, one of the only houses on the Hill that is not shoehorned in among its neighbors, and the only one with a broad driveway.

That was not the only thing that was different about television's Beacon Hill, however. The story was about an upwardly mobile Irish family in the 1920s; any time before then, or indeed since – right up until the last twenty years or so, Irish families simply did not live there.

Beacon Hill was the center of Boston society almost from the beginning when a silversmith named Paul Revere, a lawyer named James Otis, an importer named John Hancock and the richest man in the whole colony, Thomas Boylston, built small mansions there to take advantage of the view.

Today it is a neighborhood that consists of steep, narrow streets lined with townhouses, many of which have long since been subdivided into very highly priced apartments. Some ground floor shops are rented by sandal makers and poster dealers, galleries and handicraft stores. Interspersed among the Beacon Hill houses lie mansions designed by Charles Bulfinch, some of which are still occupied by Old Families. Charles Bulfinch also takes credit for the State House and just about every other important building in town. Along with them, Beacon Hill is still a symbol of wealth and privilege, a place from which one can look down on the rabble and over to the State House for help in keeping the rabble in their place.

On the whole, with reference to the series *Beacon Hill*, the upwardly mobile Irish of the '20s made their homes outside Boston, in suburbs like Brookline, Dorchester and Jamaica Plain.

Most of the houses on Beacon Hill were built and occupied by people with a high idea of their place in life long before Irish immigrants began arriving in huge numbers in the early nineteenth century. Mount Vernon Street, where the television series was filmed, is one of the best on the Hill and an absolute joy for strollers. It is a happy mix of Classical and Federal architecture with a little sprinkling of Victorian just to keep you smiling. Each building, not just on this street but all over the Hill, has a personality of its own – together they are like a Vivaldi concerto with the State House as a virtuoso solo instrument.

Wrought-iron fences and balconies soften the solid effect of stone and brick; gas lights make shadows dance on the surfaces. In summer, red geraniums and green ivy spill out of window boxes. In winter, especially at Christmas, seasonal light and warmth are breathed out through high-mullioned windows. It is city life as city life was meant to be.

One of the houses on the Hill is a little lower than the rest because the lot it stands on had been owned by the man across the street who made it a condition of its sale that no structure on it could be built more than thirteen feet high. After all, anything higher would spoil his view. Further down the block, the seller of some lots made the buyer agree to set the prospective buildings back off the street so he would not have his view of the Charles River blocked out. Who could blame either of them, but where in the world other than Boston could you find buyers who would agree to such demands?

John Hancock's house on the Hill was torn down some years ago and replaced by another, whose owners used their old address from down the street. The Architectural Commission would have saved it today, but when it was offered for sale to the state as a landmark, it was turned down because the asking price was too high.

Nearby stands the Boston Athenaeum, one of the world's great libraries. Among other things, it contains George Washington's personal book collection, each with Washington's book plate and his signature. It is a strictly private library founded by Daniel Webster and others, including Ralph Waldo Emerson's father, and is open only to the gentlemen who support it and the scholars who need it.

Gentlemen and scholars! The words go with Boston as well as clams go with beer!

It was not always the case. Back in 1624, not long after the Pilgrims had settled themselves down in Plymouth, a ship full of indentured servants arrived in Massachusetts Bay. Their leader, Thomas Morton, freed them and invited them to settle down with him in a town he called Merriemount. They were all from Elizabethan England and had quite different ideas about life than those of the Puritans who preceded them. They loved a good time. They thought it was great fun to go fishing and hunting and not do much else. As a result, the Indians adored them.

They had not been there three years when Morton decided it was time they had a big party. After all, had the Pilgrims not put together a three-day feast at harvest time a few years beforehand? May Day was the day he picked and, as a centerpiece for the party, they built an eighty-foot maypole topped with deer antlers. Then the fun began. William Bradford, of Plymouth, said in his *History* that they were "drinking and dancing about it many days together, inviting the Indean woman for their consorts, dancing and frisking togither like so many faeries, and worse practices." It sounds as if it was more fun than Thanksgiving.

It was all too much for the long-suffering Plymouth Puritans. However, they were a peaceful group, and they held their peace. Then it was discovered that the Merriemount settlers were selling guns to the Indians. The Puritans dispatched a force under the command of Captain Miles Standish to drive them back where they came from.

It ordered Morton to surrender, but he hurled back an insult instead, calling Miles Standish "Captain Shrimpe." Standish then attacked and easily defeated them. They were soon loaded on a passing ship and sent back to England. Standish admitted later that the defeat was easy because they were "over armed with drinke."

In this way, thanks to the "Demon Rum," Massachusetts Bay was made safe for God-fearing people, and it would not be long before more of them arrived.

These subsequent settlers were also Puritans like the people who had built the colony at Plymouth, but not quite. The Plymouth brand of Puritanism was a faith completely at odds with and separate from the Church of England, which they felt was far too Roman. The new settlers felt the same way, but believed they should nonetheless remain Anglicans and work from within to change the Church.

They formed a company called the Massachusetts Bay Company, which was chartered to settle and to trade, with a heavy emphasis on the latter. They arrived in the summer of 1629 and settled in a place they called Salem, meaning "house of peace."

Up until that time, most of the American colonies were run by trading companies from headquarters in London. The directors of the Massachusetts Bay Company, apparently believing their own P.R., decided to move themselves to America. That way, they had less immediate, on-site interference from the Crown and the Church. It gave them greater control over their own destiny.

Therefore, in 1630, John Winthrop, Lord of Groton Manor and head of the Massachusetts Bay Company, arrived in Salem with 400 settlers and an urge to take over. Rather than settling in Salem, which was already overcrowded, they moved down the bay and established a string of settlements, one of which they called Boston.

Within the next ten years, another 20,000 settlers followed them.

Winthrop's brand of Puritanism attracted middle and upper-class businessmen, who sold out their interests back home and, as a result, arrived with some cash in their pockets. "Send us your poor..." was not a slogan the Massachusetts Bay Company would have espoused. The newcomers' cash bought food and housing in Massachusetts and then went back to England to pay for things they needed but could not produce for themselves. Also, because they were businessmen, it was only natural they should continue to be so in the new country. In no time at all, they were trading fish for Virginia tobacco and shipping it off to England. They were shipping fish to Portugal and arranging for the boats to return loaded with wine. They had set themselves up as princes, and that made them the Establishment in Colonial America – gentlemen to the core, and scholars too, of course. One of the first things they learned was that rum was in great demand in Africa and that Africans were in great demand in the West Indies, which is where the sugar comes from to make rum. They swiftly made the connection and for a long time Boston produced more rum than any city in the world.

That, of course, is not to say that scholarship in Boston was only restricted to chasing money. The Puritans believed that anyone who could not read was, at the very least, Satan's tool and most likely doomed to damnation and hellfire. To prevent this, one of their first acts was to build a school in Boston, modeled after the ones they knew in England. They called it the Boston Latin School, and it became the model for public education all over the United States. The idea was to teach youngsters to read the Bible for themselves so that they would not be exposed to the Word by hearsay. It was only for boys, of course. Not that they did not want to keep their daughters from the Devil's clutches; but it was decided that most girls could learn to read at their mother's knee, while they were learning needlepoint and all those other essential arts. If the mother was too busy and the family rich enough, there were private schools for girls and such establishments instructed the girls in social arts, such as dancing, along with reading and writing.

The Massachusetts Bay people were even more concerned about the future of their church than the future of their children, and fretted about what might happen if the supply of preachers ran out. Every town needed one, and there were plenty of good men in England who wanted the jobs. In the long run, however, they knew they would have to develop some home-grown ministers.

One of the preachers brought over from England was

a man named John Harvard, who died within a year of arriving. He was so impressed by the idea of establishing a college that he left his library and half his fortune, about £400, for such an establishment in his will to start the ball rolling. His bequest impressed the colonists enough to name the college they established with his help after him. Even the General Court were impressed enough to match his grant from tax receipts.

The new college was established in a place called Newtown. However, probably as a gesture to give the school confidence and a tradition to live up to, the name of the town was quickly changed to Cambridge.

John Harvard probably would not recognize the place today, any more than he would recognize himself in the wonderful if unlike statue of him by Daniel Chester French. The old town common is partly preserved in Harvard Square, but new buildings from just about every period have taken up the space that was originally left between the houses. A great many fine Colonial buildings still stand in Cambridge, but even the oldest is some fifty years younger than Harvard itself. A great many of the buildings that look Colonial may have been built when your grandfather was a boy. Some of the buildings are Victorian, many are Gothic, depending on what style was in fashion when they were built.

The oldest building on the Harvard campus is the Georgian-style Massachusetts Hall, built in 1718. Its mate, Harvard Hall, was built about fifty years later. They faced onto Cambridge Common until the 1880s when Stanford White built Johnson Gate and the fence. All the great architects of America seem to have contributed to Harvard Campus, for example: Charles Bulfinch's University Hall; Ware and Van Brunt's landmark Memorial Hall; H.H. Richardson's masterpiece Sever Hall; Horace Trumbauer's Widener Library; McKim, Mead & White's Robinson Hall and William Morris Hunt's Hunt Hall. The great twentieth-century architects also claim a share of Harvard's structures, Walter Gropius being one of the earliest. Cambridge is now dotted with the work of such men as Edward D. Stone, Philip Johnson, I.M. Pei, Hugh Stubbins and others.

The first major reinforced-concrete structure ever built is to be found in Harvard, but it was not the work of a modern architect. It is the Harvard Stadium, built in 1903 to a design by Ira Nelson Hollis, a Harvard engineering professor.

Those big, white buildings visible on crossing Harvard Bridge from Boston to Cambridge are not Harvard University buildings at all but part of another proud Boston institution: the Massachusetts Institute of Technology. A few of MIT's buildings reflect the Beaux-

Arts style that was popular when the institute moved over the River from Boston in 1913, but most of them have the modern look of the work of men such as Eduardo Catalano, Hugh Stubbins, Pietro Belluschi and Emery Roth. Of course, it is what goes on inside these buildings that is really important. Much of the atom bomb development and other technology of the Second World War was developed in them, and many of the ideas that put men on the moon came from MIT scientists. Most importantly, for the rest of New England, the brainpower concentrated in Cambridge attracts industry to the area in the form of companies who need to be abreast of all the latest developments as soon as possible.

At the same time, Harvard is a center of hallowed tradition, though some of the traditions will leave outsiders scratching their heads. During the nineteenth century, it was a rule there that "no scholar shall go out of his chamber without coate, gown or cloake; and it should be modest and sober habit without strange ruffian-like or newfangled fashions, without any lavish dresse or excess of apparrell whatsoever."

There was also a rule that no freshman could wear his hat in Harvard Yard "unless it rains, hails or snows, provided he be on foot and have not both hands full."

Until relatively recently, the most obvious tradition was that Harvard was for men only. Women enrolled in Radcliffe. However, they were taught by Harvard professors, and the president of Harvard signed their diplomas, which always bore the Harvard seal. Radcliffe and Harvard finally "got married," and these days a Radcliffe girl is as much a Harvard man as anybody.

On the other side of town, Boston nurtures a special tradition that has its roots in the 1770s. The celebration of this tradition centers on a meat market called Faneuil Hall (pronounced in the same way as flannel), which was one of the buildings used by a group of hotheads as a secret meeting place in which to plan a revolution over 200 years ago. Faneuil Hall is found in Dock Square, and it is not far from the place where some of those same hotheads dumped quantities of British tea into the harbor before putting their revolutionary plans into action.

Dock Square was the city's marketplace from the very earliest times. It was where merchant ships docked, and business people knew they could eliminate the middleman if they did their dealing right there on the docks. Over the years, other markets abutted on the original to handle the overflow. The most elaborate of them, Quincy Market, has been restored recently in a twenty-million-dollar effort spanning six years. Its refurbishment has given Boston the best waterfront area east of San Francisco, bustling with an exciting combination of food shops and restaurants and merchants selling plants and cookware, books and kitchenware, wine, cheese and whatever else can be sold to a crowd of people intent on enjoying themselves.

The waterfront is based in a narrow, 550-foot-long building with a three-story copper rotunda in the middle. Pushcart vendors positioned on the wide, brick plazas either side of the rotunda are protected by glass awnings that keep the weather out but let the sunshine in. About the only thing that is missing in the Boston waterfront area, compared with other restored historic neighborhoods around the country, are the poster sellers, the candle dealers, the head shops and incense peddlers. Nobody seems to miss them much.

The Esplanade along the river gives Bostonians a place to take a breath of fresh air. Lewis Mumford described it as: "the outstanding achievement in American urban planning for the nineteenth century." Residential streets of the area are separate from shopping streets, but not separate to the point of inconvenience. This area houses commercial districts too, so Back Bay people often do not have to travel far to work. It is a neighborhood that stretches from McKim, Mead and White's magnificent Symphony Hall at one end, to the wonderful Public Gardens at the other. It also incorporates Copley Square and Commonwealth Avenue. What city would not be pleased to boast either one?

The Boston Public Library is on Copley Square. McKim, Mead & White designed the original. Philip Johnson "improved" on their work in an addition he designed in 1972. Others have also tried to improve Back Bay in recent years. The Prudential Life Insurance Company, for instance, built a complex of buildings in the 1960s that are probably best forgotten, except that the tower dominating them is so huge you can not escape it. Another insurance company, John Hancock, added its own contribution to the skyline by raising a sixty-story tower. Its architect, who is probably better left nameless, envisioned an "invisible building" covered with a reflecting glass skin. Unfortunately, variable temperatures and high winds shattered the dream, and if Bostonians valued their lives they stayed away from the "windswept plaza" at the base. If they did not get hit by flying glass, they got in the way of the sweepers. The windows that were blown out were replaced by plywood panels as a temporary measure, and the building was known as the plywood tower. The problems seem to have been solved now, but it is probably a good idea to make sure your life insurance is paid up if you plan to walk anywhere near it.

The Back Bay really was a bay when Winthrop and his company arrived. Or rather it was more like a marsh. As the city grew, some of the inlets were drained and filled in, but in the middle of the last century it was a mess. In 1857 the City Fathers built a special railroad over to Needham and, until the turn of the century, trains went back and forth over it carrying dirt to fill in the bay. When the project was finished, people began to come down from Beacon Hill and across the Common to settle there. The Charles Street edge of the Common, all the way to Washington Street, had been the shoreline up until then. New streets, such as Commonwealth Avenue – which could have been imported from Paris – added to the lure of the latest thing. By the middle of the nineteenth century, anyone who wanted to be considered fashionable in Boston had to be seen walking on Commonwealth Avenue on their way from church to a stroll through the Commons.

Boston Common is the oldest public park in the country. It was also the result of one of the first shrewd business deals by Puritans in America. When they arrived, the whole Shawmut Peninsula, where they built Boston, was owned by a preacher who was operating on a king's grant, and had lived there for nearly ten years. As a man of God, he was happy to see these God-fearing people from the old country and he invited them to stay. They took over. Oh, they were generous to him. They let him keep fifty acres, plenty of land for a man who was not even a farmer. Within a few months, just to make things legal, they asked him to sell them his fifty acres. He did, gladly, for thirty pounds. The deed he signed gave Winthrop and his company the whole peninsula. Of course, it was a low price – even considering the value of the English pound today, but it was a better deal than Peter Minuit gave the owners of Manhattan Island.

Everyone in the Colony had been levied to raise the money and, in return, the Governor decreed that what had been the preacher's garden would henceforth be common property. He was as good as his word. It still is.

At first, it was used as a pasture for the colonists' cows and a parade ground for their militia. Not much later, it was used for public executions and punishments of one sort or another. As in England at the time, a good hanging was a great crowd-pleaser. In Boston they called it going to see someone "turned off." It was also considered to be fun to stroll along the Common and toss rotten eggs at some poor soul who had been sentenced to "an hour in ye stocks." Oddly enough, the first person to fall victim to the stocks in Boston was the unfortunate carpenter who built them. The Elders thought his price was too high for the work, so they fined him the amount of his bill and locked him up for an hour.

British troops were billeted on the Common, and left from there in their attempt to reach Lexington and Concord before Paul Revere. Some of them are buried under it alongside the unfortunates who were hanged on the Common.

Though the Boston Massacre – one of the first antagonistic brushes with the British before the war – happened on State Street, the memorial to its victims stands on the Common. They say it is good luck to shake the hand of the statue of Crispus Attucks, the black man who was the first to give his life for his country in the Revolutionary War. If it is true, there are a lot of lucky people in Boston. The hand is the best-polished piece of bronze in the city.

It is said the game of football was first played on Boston Common. It was also the place where, in 1688, an event took place that would become a political football later. Goody Glover was hanged as a witch because she had been caught saying the rosary in Gaelic in front of a "graven image" of the Virgin. All Irishmen were thought to be devils. Apparently everyone in Boston believed that in 1688.

One of the things that makes Boston, and all New England for that matter, unique in America is that it existed for two centuries, and more, with only a single culture. All the English colonies in the south welcomed anybody and everybody no matter where they came from. The Dutch were the original founders of New York; Germans had flocked to Philadelphia; the French and Spanish were part of the established fabric almost everywhere – but Boston was quite content to stay English. In the first twenty years of the colony, some 20,000 people migrated there, and just about all of them came from England. Not only that, but almost all of them were Puritans dedicated with all their hearts to success, to God and to hard work, although not necessarily in that order!

As their numbers grew, so did the number of towns they lived in. But Boston was always at the heart of it, and no one ever dared challenge that. Later, as they began to industrialize, the great Boston entrepreneurs looked out into the countryside and where the poets among them saw laughing, bubbling brooks and sparkling waterfalls, they saw free energy. They changed old towns and built new ones, and for the first time farmers did not have to feel guilty about not having enough work to do in the wintertime. There was cloth to be woven, shoes to be made – there was work to be done.

There was so much work in fact, they needed more people to do it all. Then, as He had done so often before in the view of the Puritans, God provided them with an answer to the problem. In 1845, Ireland was visited by a famine that wiped out more than a million people in less than five years. Rather than starve, a million and a half of them left the country. In spite of what they may have thought of old England, New England seemed very attractive indeed, and there were jobs and opportunities there.

Within forty years, Boston had an Irish Mayor – but what a terrible forty years for the Irish they were! It was bad enough that these newcomers were Irish. One of Boston's venerable leaders wrote: "They were the scum of creation, beaten men from beaten races, representing the worst failure in the struggle for existence ... These immigrants were inferior peoples whose prolific issue threatened the very foundations of Anglo-American civilization." That was part of the rub: these new immigrants were almost all Catholics – one of the religious groups the Puritans had come to Boston to escape.

The Puritans called them "muckers" and "micks," "blacklegs" and "greenhorns." They hired their women, whom they always called "Bridget" at best, or "Biddy" at worst, to do the dirty work in their homes for one dollar fifty a week, keeping a third of this salary to pay for her board.

By the time the Irish began to arrive in Boston, the North End had already lost its cachet for fashionable Yankees, and whole neighborhoods there had simply been abandoned. Irish families moved into the big, old mansions, usually one to a room, which meant they shared what sanitary facilities there were among dozens of whole families. That, in turn, meant many of them fell victim to cholera, smallpox and worse.

However, if the Puritans thought they were the only people to whom God had given gifts, they did not know much about God or the Irish. One of the newcomers' gifts was for survival. They believed, as an article of faith, that a man's reward was in heaven. That helped them endure hardships even the toughest Yankee would have blanched at. The Puritans believed just as strongly in the here and now. Hardship for a Puritan was as much a punishment as a test.

The Irish had a gift for politics too, and they knew how to use it. As a countermeasure, the Puritans set up residency laws and literacy laws to keep them from voting, but it was only a matter of time before that trick would not work any more. They used their influence to spread stories that the Irish were nothing but drunkards, people who preferred welfare to an honest day's work and, worst of all, people who could not be loyal to any state because any information entrusted to them would be transmitted straight back to the Pope in Rome.

The old-line leaders were by and large Republican in the days after the Civil War. So the Irish were Democrats. To counter the growing opposition, Bostonians formed new parties that allowed them tighter control. One of them was called "The Know-Nothings," because its members usually did not discuss what they stood for except with insiders.

They became so powerful that they elected a governor and gained control of both the state house and the city council in a single election. It was then people discovered how little they really did know. Though they did all they could to keep the Irish down, Irish patience won out and eventually the door was open for them to play the game they love so much: running for office and getting elected.

Even had the established Bostonians had gone to the docks to meet the immigrant Irish with brass bands and CARE Packages when they first began arriving, there would probably still have been friction. In most cases, the Irish had had bad experience of the "Bloody British" back home, and their new hosts were, in many cases, more British than their cousins in Sussex. Even though without the Bostonians America might have stayed a part of the British Empire to this day, they nonetheless did not forget their English roots and remained proud of them. Then there was that problem of religion. To the Irish, being Protestant was much worse than being a heathen and, of course, the Puritans were Protestants to a fault. It was not the first time and, unfortunately, not the last, that men have used the love of God to justify hate.

By the time the Irish had gained political clout, Boston had changed again. While the political scrapping between the Irish population and the old guard was going on Italian immigrants began arriving, then Lithuanians and Poles. Germans came too, along with Portuguese, Scandinavians and French Canadians. But the Irish controlled the wards, and if anyone wanted a street light or a city job they had to go to them. After all those years of suffering the stings of racial prejudice, they began to mete them out to the newcomers. Human nature is a mysterious thing.

However, no matter what else Boston immigrants found, most eventually got what they came for: freedom.

Of all the cities in the United States, Boston stands tall in the upper ranks of those places that are good for walking. For strollers, walkers, runners, joggers, even roller skaters, Boston is their kind of town. One of the best walks in Boston is the one they call The Freedom Trail.

It begins at the Park Street side of the Common with a monument not to the Revolutionary War, but to the Civil War: the Park Street Church. Henry James called it "the most interesting mass of brick and mortar in America." The call for the abolition of slavery went out from Boston first and some of the most impassioned speeches were made from the pulpit here. Whether it was guilt over having made so much money by the slave trade, or

Puritan religious fervor, slavery was an issue all Boston responded to, and Bostonians were found among the ranks of leaders both in the abolition movement and in the Civil War. Around the corner is the Old Granary Burying Ground. It is one of five in the center of the city, and a favorite place for people who enjoy making rubbings from old headstones. You need a permit to do it, but it is worth the effort because among some of the names such enthusiasts pick up are those of John Hancock, Samuel Adams and Mother Goose. Andrew Faneuil, of Faneuil Hall fame, is resting in peace under a stone inscribed with his nephew's first initial and his own name misspelled as "Funel." Benjamin Franklin's parents are buried there too, and so is Boston's first mayor.

Why, you might well ask, is a cemetery called Granary? It was named for a huge shed that once stood next to it, built as a storehouse for surplus wheat and corn that could be distributed to the needy poor. But in the early days Boston had very few poor families and after the custodian reported that "weevils have taken the wheat, and mice annoy the corn much, being very numerous," the building was torn down and the salvage used to build a tavern. But the old name lives on, so to speak, in the cemetery.

The trail leads past the Athenaeum and into School Street, where Colonial youngsters were exposed to the three Rs and an occasional hickory stick at the Boston Latin School. At this point, strollers usually find a chance to sit down because the trail leads inside King's Chapel, which was the first Episcopal church in New England but has been a Unitarian church since Revolutionary times. As such, it was also the first Unitarian church in New England too. Much of the furnishings consist of gifts from English royalty, and its interior can be called "Georgian" with no argument from anybody. In fact, it is probably the best example of Georgian decor anywhere in New England.

The church was originally a wooden building, but the wooden frame was covered with local granite after resident architects discovered that it was a good building material. Once the new stonework shell was finished, the old frame was torn down from within.

Not far away stands the Old Corner Book Store, restored for the enjoyment of all by yet another important Boston institution, the *Boston Globe*. Emerson knew the Corner Book Store well, as did Hawthorne and Longfellow. The Old City Hall is near there too, wonderfully restored as a restaurant and office building. Not far from it another great job of restoration has preserved the Old South Meetinghouse as a bookstore and museum.

The Freedom Trail wanders past Faneuil Hall and the Quincy Market as well as the new City Hall, a massive pile of concrete and glazed brick. Then, mercifully, it takes you out of the way of an elevated expressway, a construction Boston seems to build in unfortunate abundance. From there, it wanders back into the past, coming up alongside the only extant, seventeenth-century wooden building in Boston: Paul Revere's house. When it was built, it was conveniently located next to the town pump, across from the public market, near the meeting house and hard by the local guardhouse. A lively spot indeed. Paul Revere added his own contribution to the general din: he had sixteen children. He contributed much else too, of course, and his accomplishments are detailed for anyone who visits the house to see for themselves. The style of the house is Elizabethan English, and looks just like the homes the Puritans left behind them in the old country.

Most of the old houses were destroyed in a series of fires over the early years. Fire was surely the colonists' worst enemy, and it is the reason why very few authentic Colonial buildings are still standing in any of the cities that were part of the original thirteen colonies. Urban "improvement" is another reason too, of course. There is not a single Dutch building left in New York, for instance. Most were destroyed by fire, but the last remaining one had an encounter with a wrecker's ball some years ago.

Just around the corner from Paul Revere's house, and an appropriate end to the Freedom Trail, lies Old North Church, where Paul Revere staged his famous sound and light show. It is one of the oldest churches in Boston, containing bells cast in England. For years was the highest structure in the city – made tall purposely as a landmark for sailors. It looks very like the church of St. James in Piccadilly, London, and British tourists often notice the resemblance. Londoners with longer memories recognize it as being extremely like a church that once stood on Queen Victoria Street in London. It was called St. Andrews-by-the-Wardrobe and was eventually linked with the parish of St. Ann, Blackfriars. Unfortunately, it was destroyed in the unpleasantness called the London Blitz. Some of the parishioners of North Church had come from Blackfriars, so perhaps the resemblance was more than a coincidence.

It broke sharply with a tradition of long standing in New England. The Puritans had built meeting houses that were purposely simple, undecorative and uncomfortable. This church contained a raised pulpit, galleries, divided pews and simple but quite lovely decoration. Popery? Some might have said so in 1723 when it was built, but by then even the Puritans were ready for a little style in their religion.

We call it "Old" North Church today for Longfellow's poem celebrating Paul Revere's ride. Actually, it is the newer of two structures which were called "North

Church." The other one was chopped up for firewood by British troops billeted near there. This church's official name is really Christ Church.

Nonetheless it is old, and its style was copied in churches all over New England and up and down the East Coast. Its steeple was not added until the church was more than fifteen years old – but, nevertheless, added in plenty of time to be useful to Paul Revere. Like every other steeple in New England, it was built like a telescope from inside the church. As each stage became smaller, the workmen's space grew tighter. The spire, in this case a weather vane in the shape of a pot with a flower, banner, ball and five-pointed star, was built on the ground and then pushed up through the hole in the top. Life was much safer, if more confining, for steeplejacks in those days.

A hurricane blew the steeple down in 1804 and it was replaced, with another, some fifteen feet shorter than the original, by Charles Bulfinch. The same thing happened again in 1955, and it was replaced again. This time they had to send all the way to New Hampshire for a crane high enough to replace the weather vane. So much for progress. During the Revolution, the North End was a hotbed of Tories. A great many of the residents left town and headed for Canada when they saw how things were turning out. Slightly deserted, the neighborhood became less fashionable and, that aside, people were beginning to long for the open spaces of the suburbs. They moved to Beacon Hill.

By the beginning of the nineteenth century, the North End had been transformed from Boston's most prestigious neighborhood into a industrial district full of factories, producing everything from cannon balls to flower pots. The workers in the factories, because there was no subway then, moved into the neighborhood, and they were followed by new arrivals from abroad.

Within a generation the neighborhood would be called "Little Italy," and it is one of the most tightly packed city neighborhoods anywhere in the United States. It is a section consisting of narrow streets, alleys and tenement buildings enlivened with tomato plants and basil growing in pots on fire escapes. From lines stretched between the buildings, laundry flies like the fluttering banners of some medieval festival. Old people with lined faces sit outside their buildings discussing the past and the present, punctuating each sentence with their hands.

If you can make it past Quincy Market with your appetite intact, a reward is to be found here. Stop in a groceria to take home a little homemade pasta as a souvenir of the trip. Go to a clam house for some scungilli, then next door to a trattoria for liguini, then on to a ristorante for the best veal cutlet limone this side of Naples. For the crowning touch, sit at an outdoor café under a bright red and green umbrella, treat yourself to a sinfully sweet cannoli and sip hot, strong espresso while you watch this wonderful world pass by.

Late in the summer and well into the fall, when most visitors to New England are heading for the hills to gaze on the splendid fall colors, the northeast becomes more colorful itself. It is fiesta time, and the streets are decorated with colored lights. The sidewalks are covered with stands selling pizza and ravioli, zeppole and Italian cheesecake. You can try your luck at games of chance or games of skill – it is almost impossible not to have a good time.

Festivities come to a peak on October 12, when Boston Italians come out in force to remind other Bostonians that an Italian, Christopher Columbus, made it across the ocean in 1492, a long, long time before those Pilgrims set foot on Plymouth Rock in 1620.

After World War II, a great many younger Italian families moved away from the North End and out into the suburbs. But the neighborhood itself exercises a strong lure over its old inhabitants, and some are starting to come back now that areas around it are being renewed, and repopulating the neighborhood is, of course, the best form of urban renewal there can be.

Italian opera came to Boston some years after the Italians themselves. It started seriously with a performance of *La Gioconda* as the curtain raiser for the 1907 season. It was such a hit that the cultural establishment dispatched an architect to study all the great opera houses of Europe and design a better one. Whether he succeeded or not is a matter for historians to debate. His opera house was torn down in 1958 but, while it lasted, it represented the refinement of culture *par excellence* to Bostonians, who turned up each season dressed in the finest clothes and most expensive jewels their money could buy.

The Puritans were not known for their passion for music, though some of them were known to be very good dancers. Their idea of a moving musical experience was an evening of psalm singing; and their idea of entertainment was listening to a good lecture. However, during the middle of the nineteenth century, their mood changed as they discovered Mozart and lyric poetry, Haydn and the great works of literature. Forty years later, Henry Lee Higginson founded the Boston Symphony Orchestra. He directed it and supported it with his own money from its founding in 1881 until 1918.

In Boston, they call it simply "Symphony." Socially aspiring Boston women meet their peers every Friday all winter long at the afternoon concerts in Symphony Hall. It is a ritual Lucius Beebe said takes on "the aspect of holy days dedicated to the classics and a vast craning of necks to be certain that the Hallowells and the Forbeses are in their accustomed stalls." In summer "Symphony" is at Tanglewood in the Berkshires, a tradition started by one of the orchestra's great conductors, Serge Koussevitzky, in 1936. The place he picked, which now also houses a summer music school, was the former summer home of Nathaniel Hawthorne.

For city-bound Bostonians, the Hatch Memorial Bandshell on the Charles River is where to find the sounds of summer. All during the month of July, the Boston Pops entertains in free concerts there. It is a tradition, like the orchestra itself, begun by the late Arthur Fiedler, himself one of Boston's real treasures. The Pops Concerts are held inside Symphony Hall in the spring. But the real highlight of the year for the Pops and for all of Boston is their Fourth of July concert on the River, complete with fireworks and their trademark: *The Stars and Stripes Forever*.

In summer, the grassy esplanade along the Charles River is a haven for joggers, sunbathers and lovers. At night, they stroll along Copley Plaza to listen to street musicians or sit on the steps of the Public Library, perhaps to discuss what a wonderful place this city is. Or maybe they go down to the waterfront to find a breeze and a little wine and cheese.

Office workers spend their lunch hours on the plaza outside City Hall, grabbing a snack from a sidewalk vendor and relaxing to the sounds of a bluegrass fiddle or an electric piano or both competing with each other.

It has always had the reputation of a truly livable city, but Boston may not have been more livable at any time in her history than right now. People who move there from other cities stay there. People who discover it as students keep going back to recharge their mental batteries. Quite simply, people who like cities love Boston.

It has its detractors, of course. What city does not? But people who find fault usually do not understand cities and do not care to try. One of the most common complaints heard from them is that they are not safe. Well, when someone asked the mayor of Boston if he was not worried about the possibility that places like Quincy Market might be a haven for purse-snatchers, he gave the answer the question deserved:

"If you are worried about handbag snatchers," he said, "you can live in the Berkshires."

And you'll never know what you are missing.

Previous page: the famous replica tea ship Beaver II. *Above: the Custom House Tower from Marine Park, and (facing page) John Hancock Tower. Overleaf: yachts drifting like confetti up and down the Charles River, dwarfed by the Hancock Tower. Nearby, a golden-domed spire echoes the lines of the arched central window of Copley Plaza Hotel.*

"Nail to the mast her holy flag / Set every threadbare sail / And give her the god of storms / The lightning and the gale!" These impassioned words from Oliver Wendell Holmes' stirring poem saved the USS Constitution (facing page) from being scrapped in 1830. This grand old lady, launched in 1797, ran the gauntlet of many sea battles. On August 19, 1812, she destroyed the British frigate Guerrière in thirty minutes. Cannonballs bounced off her hull during the battle, earning her the fond nickname "Old Ironsides." The bolts fastening her timbers, and the copper sheathing on her undersides were made by Paul Revere. She now lies moored at the Navy Yard. Above: the Christian Science Center, and (overleaf) Boston by winter night.

"In whatever part of the world you may meet with him you can tell a Bostonian a mile off. The Bostonian knows that his own is pre-eminently the historic city of America, and he feels that no small part of its worldwide renown has descended to him as his peculiar inheritance." Samuel Adams Drake wrote these words in 1900, and even today they ring true of this gracious city of Boston. It was built up from small beginnings through canny exploitation of the sea by the Puritan settlers, who forged trade links worldwide, even finding a lucrative market for dried cod in the Roman Catholic Mediterranean … whatever they may have thought about the Pope, they greatly profited from his Friday prohibition of meat. Right: the Back Bay area of the city, reclaimed from Charles River Basin at the end of the last century. Overleaf: Longfellow Bridge, linking historic Beacon Hill with Cambridge.

In the Senate Chamber (above) of the State House (these pages and overleaf) hangs the gilded, hand-carved symbol of the state's original source of wealth: the "Sacred Cod." It may seem an odd symbol to some, and strange to find a large fish hanging in the Senate Chamber, but Davy Crockett thought not, saying, "It was quite natural to me, for at home I have at one end of my house the antlers of a noble buck and the heavy paws of a bear." The Chamber also contains the first weapon captured from a British soldier in the Revolution. The plans for this elegant building were submitted by Charles Bulfinch only a few years after independence had been won, and its cornerstone was laid in 1795 by those two notable revolutionaries Samuel Adams and Paul Revere. Revere also supplied the copper sheets for its dome, which were replaced in 1874 by gold leaf. Top: the House of Representatives.

Left and overleaf: the grand, Renaissance-style First Church of Christ, Scientist – the mother church of the Christian Science Church. It was built of Indiana limestone in 1894. The Christian Science movement itself dates from 1866, when a frail, forty-five-year-old woman called Mary Baker Patterson, later Eddy, slipped and fell heavily while walking home from a temperance meeting in Lynn, north of Boston. She focused her mind on the New Testament and, several days later, she was suddenly healed of her injuries and of the long-term illness which had plagued her youth. Some years after that she started to heal others, and the Christian Science Church had begun.

When Paul Revere bought his house (above) in 1770 it was already ninety years old. It is now the oldest house left in Boston. It was from here, on April 18, 1775, that he left on his historic ride to Lexington. The Old State House (facing page), Boston's oldest public building, dates from 1713. Here, said John Adams, "the child Independence was born" through the eloquence of men such as James Otis – so compelling was he that a visitors' gallery had to be added in 1766. The Declaration of Independence was read from its balcony on July 18, 1776, and afterwards the statues of the unicorn and the lion on the roof – symbols of British power – were tossed into the street and burned. Reproductions now stand in their place. Boston Common (overleaf) was originally the home of the Reverend William Blaxton, who invited John Winthrop's beleaguered Puritans to join him there in 1630. He then regretted his invitation, it is said, and rode off to Rhode Island on a bull, but he came back to Boston twenty-five years later to find himself a wife.

The Public Garden (left, above, right and overleaf) on Charles Street was America's first botanical garden, protected by a law that ardent conservationists had passed to prevent the erection of any building other than a city hall between Arlington and Charles streets. It was landscaped a year later, in 1860, by George F. Meacham. The Swan Boats are one of the Garden's most famous sights. They conduct rides on the man-made lake constructed out of what was once the swampy marshland of the Charles River. The bronze of George Washington (overleaf) by Thomas Ball has stood in the Public Garden since 1869. Boston's famous baseball team, the Red Sox, are based at Fenway Park (remaining pictures).

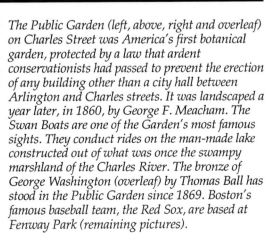

47

This page: the Old Granary Burial Ground. Founded in 1660, it grew to accommodate 1,600 graves, including those of some of America's most illustrious historical figures. Three signatories of the Declaration of Independence, John Hancock, Samuel Adams and Robert Paine, lie here, as do Peter Faneuil, Paul Revere and the five men killed in the Boston Massacre. A twenty-foot-tall, granite obelisk (below) marks the grave of Benjamin Franklin's parents. The modest stone originally laid by Franklin was replaced by it in 1827. Copp's Hill Burying Ground (facing page), the second-oldest burial ground in the city, was begun in 1659. The Charles River is the seam that joins Boston and Cambridge. Overleaf: a scull, like a water-skating insect, slips past the Weld Boathouse in Cambridge toward Anderson Bridge. Behind the Boathouse stands a famous symbol of Harvard, Eliot House with its turquoise cupola. Lowell House, surmounted by another blue cupola, contains a carillon of seventeen bells which originally came from Danilov Monastery in Moscow, complete with a Russian bell tuner. When he started to tune them by filing their rims President Lowell, thinking he was damaging them, abruptly stopped him. The Russian felt persecuted and began to believe moreover that he was being poisoned. He drank ink as an antidote ... a strangely appropriate choice of cure since Harvard is metaphorically dedicated to the "drinking in" of ink as an antidote to ignorance.

50

Left: an aerial view of North End and its two best-loved churches, golden-capped St. Stephens Church and the Old North Church with its tapering spire. St. Stephens is the only church in Boston by Charles Bulfinch that still stands. Originally its gilt dome was covered with copper supplied by Paul Revere, who also cast the bells. Old North Church, or Christ Church, was built in 1723. Its sexton, Robert Newman, following instructions given to him by Paul Revere, hung two lanterns from its 190-foot steeple on the night of April 18, 1775. In doing so he alerted patriots in Charlestown that the British were sailing to raid Concord from Boston Common rather than taking the land crossing over Boston Neck. As a boy, Revere rang the bells of Old North Church, bells which were installed in 1745 and have rung out every significant event in American history since. Overleaf: the area of the city bordering Back Bay.

Above: Marine Park and the Custom House Tower, once Boston's tallest building. Facing page bottom: the Christian Science Center. Boston City Hall (facing page top), built by Kallman, McKinnell and Knowles, has been described as "an Aztec temple on a brick desert." Overleaf: evening sun reflects off a tall, many-windowed building, making it look like a stack of gold bars mirrored in the rippled Charles River.

The Massachusetts Institute of Technology (above) boasts great facilities for experiment, including five high-energy accelerators, a large nuclear reactor and a noted nuclear engineering laboratory. So good are the facilities, and so open to individual student research projects are they, that MIT students were among the first scientists to attempt to recreate the controversial test-tube fusion experiments of Dr. Martin Fleischman in 1989. A small group, while debating the issue, spontaneously decided to try the reaction during the night after Fleischman had announced his findings to the world. Top: the Museum of Fine Arts, and (facing page) the splendid courtyard of the Isabella Stewart Gardner Museum. Overleaf: on a crisp evening the Hancock Tower rises like a slab of ice behind Longfellow Bridge.

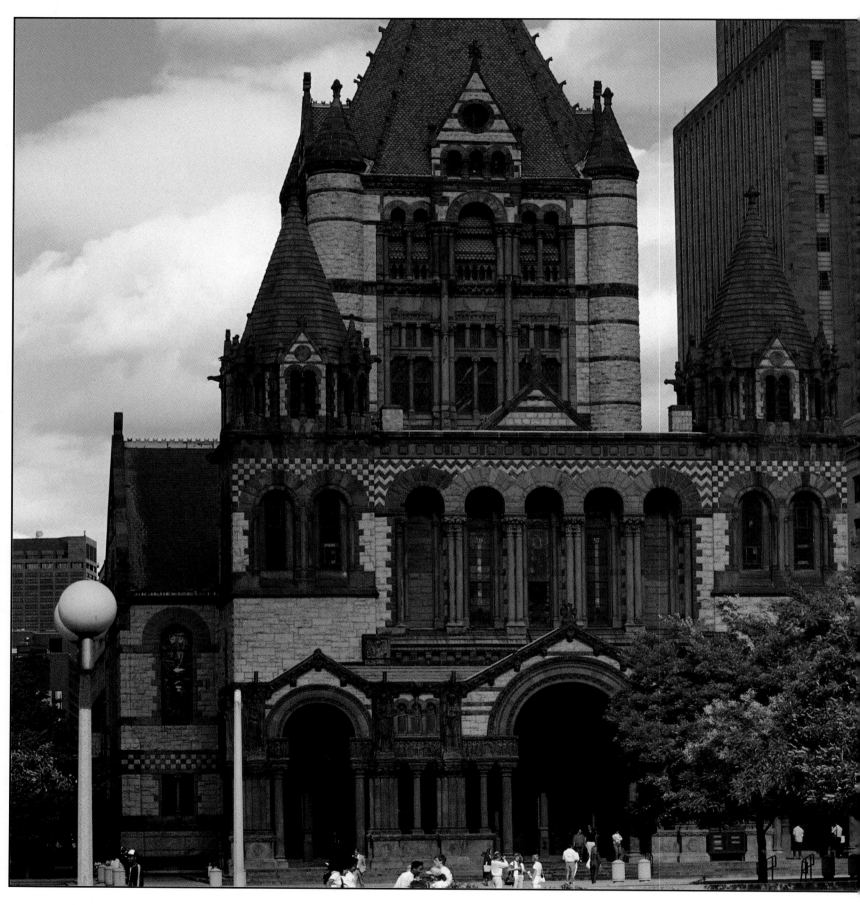

Trinity Church (these pages) was built between 1873 and 1877, and is generally thought to be Henry Richardson's masterpiece. Its design initiated the Romanesque Revival in America with what Richardson described as its "free rendering of the French Romanesque." Richardson studied at the École des Beaux Arts in Paris and was very clearly influenced by European architecture. For example, the Trinity Church tower was inspired by the Old Cathedral in Salamanca, Spain. Richardson hired John La Farge to decorate the interior. La Farge painted lavish frescoes throughout the building and made extensive use of unusual and lovely stained glass, which he designed and had made. Top right: the paneled ceiling of the tower.

Top: the interior of the New Old South Church. This church was built in 1875 in a style which is ponderously known as Anglo-Ruskinian Gothic. Above and facing page: the First Church of Christ, Scientist and the Christian Science Center. The Church is dedicated, in the words of its founder Mary Baker Patterson to reinstating "primitive Christianity and its element of healing." Overleaf: Cambridge. Cambridge was first settled in 1630 as New Towne by the Massachusetts Bay Company. In 1638, after the establishment there of Harvard College, it was renamed for the famous university town of Cambridge, England. If the new name was meant to inspire students to greater scholastic heights, it certainly worked. Harvard put Cambridge, Massachusetts, on the world's academic map.

The shop fronts of Beacon Hill (these pages) have a carefully preserved nineteenth-century air about them. However, Beacon Hill was not always so genteel. During the eighteenth century it was the site of sailors' haunts, ropewalks and bawdy houses, and was known as "Mount Whoredom" – a place calculated to raise many a Puritan eyebrow. During the nineteenth century it was home to a large black community, and many monuments of Black Bostonian history are to be found here. Among them, on Beacon Street, is the Shaw Monument, recalling the all-black 54th Massachusetts Regiment led by a twenty-six-year-old, white officer named Colonel Robert Gould Shaw. They were featured in an acclaimed film, Glory. One of Shaw's men, Sergeant William Carney, was the first black man to win the Congressional Medal of Honor.

Overleaf: Chestnut Street, Beacon Hill (these pages). Chestnut Street has housed many illustrious Americans. For instance, from 1863 to 1865, Number 13 was the home of Julia Ward Howe, the lyricist of "The Battle Hymn of the Republic," and Edwin Booth lived at 29A. Numbers 13 to 17 were designed for three sisters by Charles Bulfinch. Oliver Wendell Holmes described Beacon Hill as the abode of the "Boston Brahmins ... with their houses by Bulfinch, their monopoly of Beacon Street, the ancestral portraits and Chinese porcelain, humanitarianism, Unitarian faith in the march of mind, Yankee shrewdness and New England exclusiveness." Someone else, less eloquently, remarked that in Boston you could not shoot off a pistol without bringing down the author of a three-volume work.

Top left: Beacon Street, in the words of Oliver Wendell Holmes, "the sunny street that holds the sifted few." Left: Louisburg Square. Louisa May Alcott lived on this square at Number 10, and Jenny Lind, the "Swedish Nightingale," married her accompanist Otto Goldschmidt at Number 20 Louisburg Square while on an American tour in 1852. Above: numbers 11, 13 and 15, Chestnut Street.

Above and overleaf: the USS Constitution, *better known as "Old Ironsides." This ship was built in 1797 and took part in forty sea battles, emerging victorious from all of them. She has since been completely refurbished; less than ten percent of her timbers are original. Facing page:* Beaver II. *Samuel Adams' cry, "Who knows how tea will mingle with salt water?" inspired a revolutionary brew on the evening of December 16, 1773. From Griffin Wharf, three clippers loaded with chests of English tea were relieved of their cargo, which was tipped into Boston Harbor. John Adams wrote in his diary, "This destruction of the tea is so bold, so daring, so firm, intrepid and inflexible, and it must have important consequences" History, of course, proved him right.* Beaver II, *a Danish brig, was launched in 1908 and has now been fitted out as one of the original three tea clippers to become the main draw of the Boston Tea Party Ship and Museum.*

Right: the New England Aquarium on Central Wharf, with Long Wharf in the background. Overleaf: Long Wharf with the distinctive, white tower of the Custom House in Boston's Waterfront area (these pages and overleaf). The Aquarium boasts what is reputed to be the largest seawater fish tank in the world. Long Wharf, at one time 800 feet in length, extended from the Old State House to the deepest part of the harbor. The stepped, triangular, red-brick building that now stands on it is the Boston Marriott Hotel.

Left: Faneuil Hall, and (overleaf) Quincy Market. "Here Orators in ages past have mounted their attack / Undaunted by proximity of sausage on the rack." The upper floor of Faneuil Hall, "the Cradle of Liberty" and subject of Hack's verse, once reverberated to the revolutionary rhetoric of Samuel Adams and James Otis, to name but two. Later oratory was that of impassioned abolitionists. In December 1839, a meeting was planned to remember and abhor the death in 1837 of Elijah P. Lovejoy, an Illinois abolitionist murdered while protecting his printing press from an enraged mob. The mayor refused to allow the gathering to use Faneuil Hall, evoking this thunderous response from Wendell Phillips: "When Liberty is in danger, Faneuil Hall has the right, it is her duty, to strike the key-note for the United States." Today's building is the third hall, a renovation of Bulfinch's 1806 building.

Above, top and overleaf: Quincy Market, and (facing page) Faneuil Hall Marketplace. This area was, and is still, Boston's thriving commercial hub. Today stores, stalls, cafés, restaurants and barrows provide a bazaar-like feast for the senses. Smells of fresh flowers, ground coffee, baking and gourmet cooking mingle in the air.

Although Lincoln Steffens once said "I hate Boston. I don't know why … The general spirit is so far, far, far back that it gets on my nerves," the city now vies with any for modernity. But, nonetheless, freeways (left) and high-rise buildings (these pages and overleaf) cannot obscure the town's history. That would be impossible. "This town has a history," as Ralph Waldo Emerson explained. "It is not an accident, not a windmill, or a railroad station, or a cross-roads town, but a seat of humanity, of men of principle, obeying sentiment and marching to it …"

Above: Buckman Tavern, Lexington, where Minute Men gathered in response to Revere's famous alarm. About seventy-seven men lined up on the Green to face Major Pitcairn. Captain John Parker is reputed to have said to his American force, "Stand your ground. Don't fire unless fired upon, but if they mean to have a war, let it begin here." Top: Harvard Yard lying behind a gate on which is stated, "Enter to Grow in Wisdom." Charles Street Meeting House (facing page) provided a platform for the abolitionists Wendell Phillips, William Lloyd Garrison and Frederick Douglass. Overleaf: Harvard's University Hall and the Daniel Chester French "Statue of Three Lies." Its inscription reads "John Harvard, Founder, 1638." Firstly, Harvard was a benefactor, not the founder. Secondly, the college was founded in 1636. Thirdly, nobody knows what John Harvard looked like.

1775

NINETEENTH
OF
APRIL
—
1875

Above and overleaf: North Bridge, Concord. On this bridge, a reconstruction of the original, British soldiers fired on American militiamen, killing two of them. The return fire, spurred by Major John Buttrick crying "Fire, fellow soldiers, for God's sake, fire!", was thought to constitute the first American shots of the Revolutionary War. It is commemorated in an ode by Emerson: "By the rude bridge that arched the flood / Their flag to April's breeze unfurled / Here once the embattled farmers stood / And fired the shot heard round the world." The statue, Minute Man *(above), was Daniel Chester French's first important commission. Facing page: Revolutionary Monument and First Parish Church, Lexington Green.*

Below: the house in the Boston suburb of Brookline where John F. Kennedy was born. Right: Longfellow House, Cambridge. George Washington lived here from 1775 to 1776, and Longfellow rented rooms in the house while he was Professor of Modern Languages at Harvard. When he married Fanny Appleton in 1843, her father made them a present of the house and its land. Fanny died in the house in 1861 following a heart-rending accident in which her dress caught fire and her entire body was burnt, despite Longfellow's frantic attempts to put out the blaze. She died the day after the accident. Longfellow wrote Evangeline (1847), The Song of Hiawatha (1855), *and* The Courtship of Miles Standish (1858) *in this house, using quill pens and an inkstand given to him by the English poet Samuel Taylor Coleridge. Overleaf: Cambridge, linked to Boston by the John W. Weeks Bridge.*

Above: Deacon Street, and (facing page) the russet pyramid of Trinity Church Tower to the left of tail-light-streaked Boylston Street. Overleaf: the Community Boat House on the banks of the Charles River Basin near Longfellow Bridge. The dark dome further upwater is the Hatch Memorial Shell under which the Boston Pops play on summer evenings.

Above: The Wayside, and (top left) Orchard House, both in Concord. Left: Longfellow's Wayside Inn, Sudbury. These houses knew an interchange of literary residents. The Wayside was home both to the Alcotts, from 1845 to 1848, and to Hawthorne, who bought the property just after he had published The Blithedale Romance *in 1852. Much of* Little Women *is drawn from Louisa May Alcott's memories of her youth in this house, to which Hawthorne added the tower. The Alcotts also lived in Orchard House from 1858 to 1877 – the period during which Louisa wrote* Little Women *and* Little Men *– before moving to Boston. Longfellow's Wayside Inn was probably built in 1700 and claims to be the oldest operating inn in the country. Longfellow made it famous in his collection* Tales of a Wayside Inn, *the most famous poem in which remains "Paul Revere's Ride." Overleaf: Lake Cochituate.*

Right: Massachusetts Institute of Technology, and (overleaf) the grid of charming leafy squares that is Harvard University. MIT was established in 1861 by William Barton Rogers, a natural scientist, and is dedicated to the practical appliance of knowledge. Students have likened the MIT academic experience to the shock of trying to take a short drink from a gushing fire hydrant. Harvard, founded in 1636, just six years after the Massachusetts Bay Colony was established, has been a rich lode of American talent throughout its history. Poets as diverse as Longfellow and Thomas Stearns Eliot have graced its roll. Ralph Waldo Emerson, ee cummings, Robert Frost, Henry David Thoreau and Henry James were all graduates of Harvard. Anne Sullivan, the famous teacher of Helen Keller, was a graduate from Radcliffe, class of 1904. Moreover Harvard has six presidents to its credit. So perhaps it is unsurprising that Oliver Wendell Holmes, another Harvard alumnus, felt entitled to say, "All I claim for Boston is that it is the thinking center of the continent, and therefore of the planet."

Boston's gold is intellectual, historical, architectural, political and commercial. Indeed, perhaps the abiding impression left by this town in the minds of its visitors and friends is of gold: evening gold reflected in the Charles River (left); gold shining from within Boston's high-rise buildings (overleaf), and, perhaps most significantly, the morning gold of Charles Bulfinch's State House (following page), crowning Beacon Hill and the State of Massachusetts.

INDEX

Back Bay 30, 31, 56, 57
Beacon Hill 72, 73, 74, 75
Beacon Street 78
Beaver II 21, 81
Boston City Hall 59
Boston Common 44, 45
Boston Marriott Hotel 86, 87
Boylston Street 112
Brookline 108
    Birthplace of John F. Kennedy 108
Cambridge 52, 53, 62, 70, 71, 100, 102, 103, 108, 109, 110, 111, 120, 121, 122, 123
    Harvard 52, 53, 122, 123
    Harvard Yard 100
    Longfellow House 108, 109
    Massachusetts Institute of Technology 62, 120, 121
    University Hall 102, 103
    Weld Boathouse 52, 53
Charles Street Meeting House 101
Chestnut Street 76, 77, 78, 79

Christian Science Center 26, 38, 39, 40, 41, 59, 68, 69
Community Boathouse 114, 115
Concord 104, 106, 107, 116, 117
    Minute Man 104
    North Bridge 104, 106, 107
    Orchard House 116
    The Wayside 116, 117
Copp's Hill Burying Ground 51
Custom House Tower 23, 58, 86, 87
Deacon Street 113
Faneuil Hall 88, 89
Faneuil Hall Marketplace 93
Fenway Park 47
Hatch Memorial Shell 114, 115
Isabella Stewart Gardner Museum 63
John Hancock Tower 22, 24, 25, 60, 61, 64, 65
Lake Cochituate 118, 119
Lexington 100, 104, 105
    Buckman Tavern 100
    First Parish Church 105

    Revolutionary Monument 105
Long Wharf 84, 85, 86, 87
Longfellow Bridge 32, 33, 64, 65, 96
Louisburg Square 78
Marine Park 23, 58
Museum of Fine Arts 62
New England Aquarium 84, 85
New Old South Church 68
North End 54, 55
Old Granary Burial Ground 50
Old North Church 54, 55
Old State House 43
Paul Revere's House 42
Public Garden 46, 47, 48, 49
Quincy Market 90, 91, 92, 94, 95
St. Stephen's Church 54, 55
State House 34, 35, 36, 37, 128
Sudbury 116
    Longfellow's Wayside Inn 116
Trinity Church 66, 67, 112
USS Constitution 27, 80, 82, 83